I0463204

This book is based on facts and figures and is produced in collaboration with a number of Top Earners from all walk of life and different Direct Selling companies.

Legitimate companies want to make it easy and inexpensive for a person to start. Start-up costs are generally modest and are often less than $100. Your risk for starting your own business is very low!

We would like to thank all people involved for their expertise and support!

Contents

Do you have an open mind?

Direct Selling is an unknown area for 99% of all people.

This book gives you in a nutshell the information you need to get well informed on Direct Selling, based on facts and not on hype. **Lack of information is the main reason why people unnecessary fail in any business.**

About 20,000 people worldwide are earning more than $5,000+ a month and outperforming the earnings in the "corporate world". About 3 million people earn $50 - $5,000 a month. Not bad for a business you can set up part time from your home...

There are as many different reasons for joining Direct Selling businesses as there are individual stories.

You can build your business the way you want, creating your schedule to fit your lifestyle.

Celebrity endorsements

- **Warren Buffet**, owns MLM company Pampered Chef.
- **Bill Clinton**, former USA President , endorse Direct Selling.
- **Tony Blair**, former UK Prime Min., endorse Direct Selling.
- **Michael Gorbatsjov**, former Russia President.
- **Sir Richard Branson**, former owner of Vie At Home.
- **Donald Trump**, owns a Direct Selling Company.
- **Robert Kiyosaki**, one of the best motivational trainers.
- **Paul Zane Pilzer,** world-renowned economist.
- **AC Milan**, Soccer club sponsored by Amway.
- **FC Barcelona**, Soccer club sponsored by Herbalife.

Top 25 Earners

The average Top Earner in Direct Selling is earning **$21,655** per month or **$259,868** per year, based on 6,000 distributor rankings.

Over 250 distributors are making $1 million a year

Rank	Country	Est. Month	Est. Year
1	USA	$950,000	$11,400,000
2	Taiwan	$850,000	$10,200,000
3	USA	$592,000	$7,104,000
4	USA	$475,000	$5,700,000
5	Malaysia	$450,000	$5,400,000
6	USA	$425,000	$5,100,000
7	USA	$400,000	$4,800,000
8	Taiwan	$400,000	$4,800,000
9	Germany	$375,000	$4,500,000
10	USA	$350,000	$4,200,000
11	USA	$350,000	$4,200,000
12	USA	$350,000	$4,200,000
13	USA	$350,000	$4,200,000
14	Germany	$350,000	$4,200,000
15	Germany	$350,000	$4,200,000
16	USA	$350,000	$4,200,000
17	Japan	$350,000	$4,200,000
18	USA	$340,000	$4,080,000
19	USA	$300,000	$3,600,000
20	USA	$300,000	$3,600,000
21	USA	$300,000	$3,600,000
22	Japan	$300,000	$3,600,000
23	Guatemala	$300,000	$3,600,000
24	USA	$300,000	$3,600,000
25	USA	$300,000	$3,600,000

Top Earners $1 Million+ per year

Tom & Bethany Alkazin – USA, Vemma

Steve Thompson – USA, Zrii

Matt Morris – USA, Worldventures

Steve & Melyn Campbell – USA, Exfuze

Share your experience

According to the World Federation of Direct Selling Associations (WFDSA), consumers benefit from Direct Selling because of the convenience and service it provides.

By far the majority of Direct Selling companies use a multi-level compensation plan, where the member is paid not only for their own sales, but also a percentage of the sales of other representatives they introduce into the organization.

Often Direct Selling is used to introduce products or services with a high added value which has to be explained to a customer. People often ask: Why is this product not available in a retail store?

One of the reasons is that fixed stores often do not have the time to explain a product or service. The endorsement & recommendation of a Direct Seller already having great experience with a product/ service is highly appreciated. **Sharing the experience is a great benefit for Direct Sellers.** It has and will build large organizations, which benefits the people involved.

Why Direct Selling?

Direct Selling offers:

- The opportunity to own a business of your own.
- A part-time or full-time income stream.
- Personal development and low operation costs.
- Offers flexible schedules and meet new friends.
- No employees to hire.
- Very little or no capital investment.
- Work with positive people.
- Set your own goals and determine yourself how to reach them.
- The residual income component.

Direct Selling asks for:

- A certain level of communication skills.
- A couple of hours per week to start.
- The will to learn and teach others.

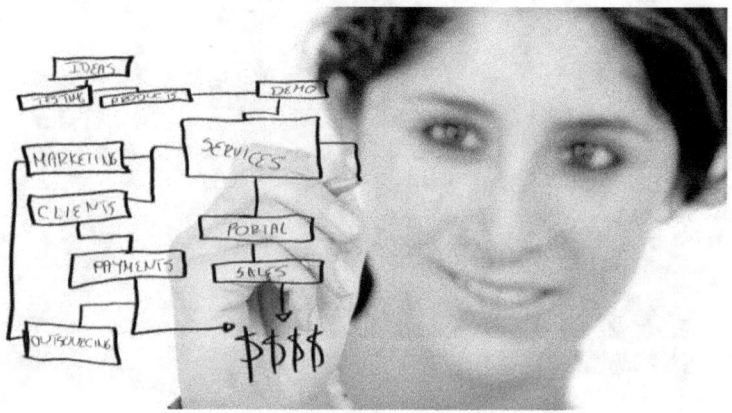

The Direct Selling Market

Direct selling is a rapidly expanding worldwide business model for the marketing of products and services directly to consumers.

There are thousands of companies with a Direct Selling model, 95% are using a Multi Level Marketing plan. The 10 largest companies have had a combined revenue of $35 billion in 2009.

The 2008-2009 financial crises have had little impact on the industry.

Company revenue in billions:

Company	Year Establish	Revenue 2007	Revenue 2008	Revenue 2009
Avon	1886	$9,938	$10,690	$10,400
Amway	1959	$7,100	$8,200	$8,400
FLP	1978	$2,000	$2,500	$3,000
Mary Kay	1971	$2,400	$2,450	$2,500
Herbalife	1980	$2,145	$2,359	$2,324
Primerica	1977	$2,200	$2,200	$2,200
Tupperware Brands	1938	$1,980	$2,160	$2,128
Natura Cos. SA	1969	$1,900	$1,900	$1,900
Nu Skin	1984	$1,157	$1,247	$1,331
Oriflame	1967	$1,109	$1,319	$1,318
Total		**$31,929**	**$35,025**	**$35,501**

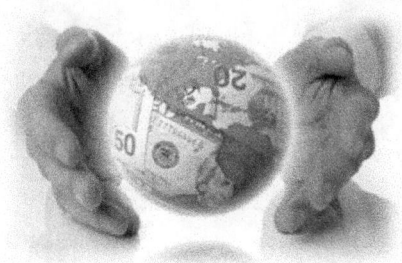

Top Earners $1 Million+ per year

Ben Sturtevant – USA, Lightyear Wireless

Jordan Adler – USA, Send Out Cards

Jonathan Budd – USA

Mike Dillard – USA

Building Residual Income

One of the advantages of Direct Selling is the possibility to earn residual income through a down line. Residual income is money you continue to make from distributors revenue in your down line.

You can be rewarded for the revenue of people you introduce and people they introduce.

Below is an example of a possible down line growth scenario.

You introduce new distributors, and so will they do:

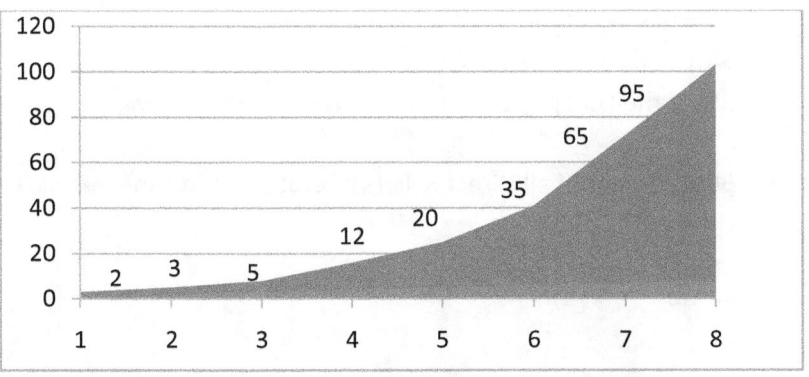

Month	Distributors	Month	Distributors
1	2	5	20
2	3	6	35
3	5	7	65
4	12	8	95

The larger your down line, the higher your down line revenue.

Facts

- The youngest Top Earner is **18** years old.
- The oldest Top Earner is **82+** years old.

- **77 %** of sales are done face-to-face.
- **11 %** of sales are through the Internet.
- **9 %** of sales are by phone.

- **74%** of US adults have purchased products from a direct seller.

- **70%** of direct sellers are woman.
- **30%** of direct sellers are men.
- **5%** of the USA population is involved in Direct Selling.

- **90%** percent of all Direct Sellers operate their businesses part-time.

Worldwide Country Revenue

Nr.	Country	Year	Revenue in Milion	Distributors
1	United States	2007	$30,800	15,100,000
2	Japan	2006	$20,390	2,700,000
3	Brazil	2008	$10,100	2,200,000
4	South Korea	2007	$9,000	3,187,933
5	Germany	2007	$8,865	778,000
6	Mexico	2007	$3,986	1,900,000
7	United Kingdom	2007	$3,564	419,500
8	Italy	2008	$3,368	365,000
9	Russia	2008	$2,866	4,413,918
10	France	2007	$2,393	223,000
11	Malaysia	2006	$2,060	4,000,000
12	Taiwan	2007	$1,700	4,530,000
13	Thailand	2006	$1,363	4,100,000
14	Colombia	2007	$1,200	771,360
15	Canada	2008	$1,180	608,778
16	Argentina	2007	$992	765,000
17	Venezuela	2006	$887	980,000
18	Turkey	2007	$864	649,000
19	Guatemala	2006	$859	39,664
20	Poland	2007	$854	670,000

Worldwide Country Revenue 2

Nr.	Country	Year	Revenue in Million	Distributors
21	Australia	2008	$844	420,000
22	Spain	2007	$747	144,000
23	South Africa	2007	$708	934,000
24	India	2006	$691	1,400,000
25	Indonesia	2007	$669	5,779,226
26	Ukraine	2007	$449	708,347
27	Chile	2007	$435	240,000
28	Sweden	2007	$400	100,000
29	Philippines	2006	$378	1,906,172
30	Switzerland	2003	$355	6,885
31	CzechRepublic	2007	$326	218,143
32	Singapore	2007	$325	575,000
33	Romania	2007	$300	210,000
34	Ecuador	2007	$280	250,000
35	Finland	2007	$251	96,000
36	Hungary	2007	$203	240,155
37	Hong Kong	2008	$191	115,500
38	Norway	2007	$160	60,000
39	Denmark	2007	$149	80,000
40	Netherlands	2005	$148	46,576

Top Earners $1 million+ per year

Daniel Müller– Germany, Unicity

Ruth Elliot – USA , Vemma

Holton Buggs – USA, Organo Gold

Carsten Ledule – Germany, PM International

Worldwide Country Revenue 3

Nr.	Country	Year	Revenue in Milion	Distributors
41	New Zealand	2008	$136	140,000
42	Portugal	2007	$89	35,391
43	Belgium	2007	$87	14,231
44	Ireland	2007	$60	17,000
45	Croatia	2007	$55	54,332
46	Slovenia	2007	$52	41,500
47	Dominican Rep.	2006	$51	73,250
48	Lithuania	2006	$49	26,000
49	Uruguay	2007	$42	43,000
50	Estonia	2007	$36	31,000
51	Latvia	2007	$35	30,000
52	Panama	2006	$31	12,500
	Total		**$116,023**	**62,449,361**

Worldwide Distributor Growth

Growth Distributors in millions worldwide

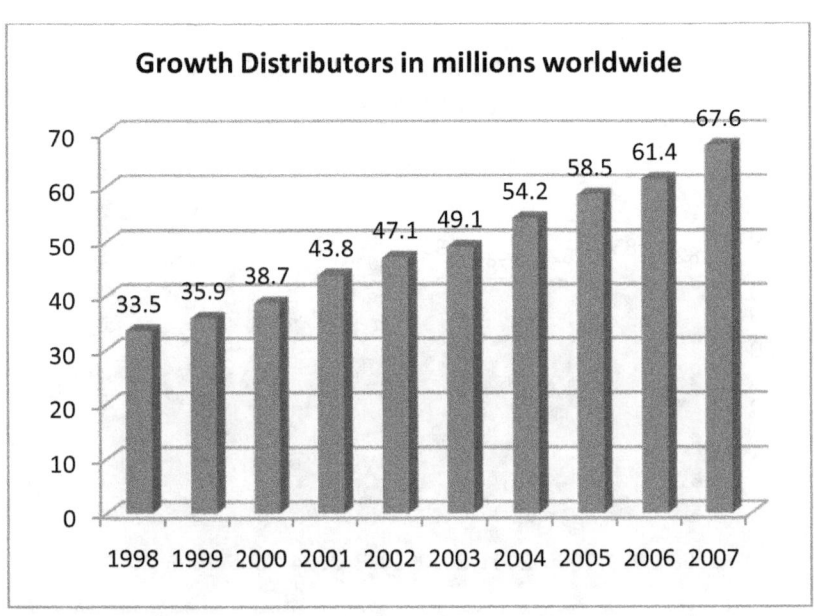

33.5	35.9	38.7	43.8	47.1	49.1	54.2	58.5	61.4	67.6
1998	1999	2000	2001	2002	2003	2004	2005	2006	2007

67 million people are involved in Direct Selling

Worldwide Growth Revenue

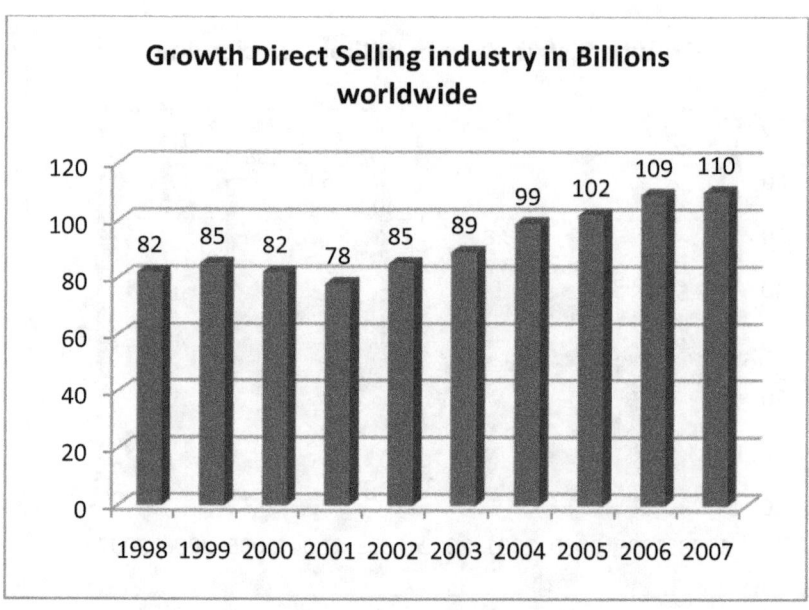

Growth Direct Selling industry in Billions worldwide

Year	Value
1998	82
1999	85
2000	82
2001	78
2002	85
2003	89
2004	99
2005	102
2006	109
2007	110

In 10 years from $82 billion to $110 billion...

Top Earners $1 million+ per year

Kathy Robbins & Paula Pritchard
USA, MXI Xocai

Brad & Marcia Hager– USA, Zrii

Sharron Sharif – USA, Xango

Myths & Misconceptions

Myth: "You have to recruit your friends and family"

Recruitment is done by the army. You are looking for a business partner. You decide who to work with. It can be anybody.

In Direct Selling you are independent; it is your business, you decide with whom to work with.

You can set it up through your warm market (people you know) market or cold market
(the rest of the world).

About 30% of the business partners are introduced through the warm market, 70% through the cold market.

Sponsoring is about taking personal responsibility for new participants in the business, ensuring they have a good understanding of the responsibilities associated with owning their own business.

Sponsoring is about caring and education.

It creates a win/win relationship between the sponsor and the enrollee.

Myth: "It looks like a pyramid"

Many people have the wrong idea of what Direct Selling is, the truth is that the business has evolved significantly in the last ten years. Pyramids are not on major stock exchanges....

If direct selling was a pyramid, 65 million people would be in prison. Direct sellers are backed up by legal companies.

In any situation you have people above you. For example sports, a company, in church, and in your social life. The beauty of Direct Selling is that you're up line wants you to be successful and will assist you if you ask for.

If you are not successful they will not get a small percentage over your success, however you will earn more over your efforts.

Myth: "Direct sellers who drop out are stuck with the inventory they purchased"

Most companies repurchase inventory purchased in the past 12 months for at least 90% of the purchase price if a direct seller decides to leave the business.

"I know somebody who failed"

As with all business or in life people fail sometimes. Getting involved is not a guarantee for success. Many people play football, not everybody is playing professional.

Talk with people who are successful in Direct Selling, they love to share their story.

If you want to become a successful football player the best thing to do is to talk with a champion and not with somebody who left the match.....

Connect with the leaders, make new friends.

This is not very effective...

Income streams

Over 50% of direct sellers report that their net income from direct selling, after taxes and expenses, is positive.

Whether you are a career builder or a stay-at-home mom or seeking a more fulfilling work experience, you will find that direct selling people support one another and create friendships that often last a lifetime.

89% of direct sellers rate their personal experience in direct selling as excellent, very good, or good.

About 80% like to use the products only, 20% is interested in the products plus the business opportunity and take the business to a professional level.

The Direct Selling business is fueled by rewarding success.

Can you do it?

People from all walks of life setup Direct Selling business with great success:

- Homeless people & entrepreneurs
- Stay at Home moms & full time corporate workers
- Teachers & students
- Doctors & unemployed
- Shop keepers & accountants
- Retired people & top sport officials
- Millionaires & broke people
- Young & old people
- Men & women

Yes, you can if you want!

Top Earners $1 million+ per year

Brian McClury– USA, Ambit Energy

Adam Green– USA, Xocai

Onyx Coale– USA, Monavie

Todd Hartog– USA, Monavie

How to start

Experienced Direct Selling leaders will tell you that to be successful, you need to choose a product or service in which you really believe and use yourself.

Get grip on the basics. Order some products, set up your (replicated corporate) website, get familiar with the products and company facts and figures.

Some people fail and quit in the first month because they are not able to understand the basics of the business. Take a week or so to learn more about the company, products and services.

Without any education you are like a bakery that is producing bread without any knowledge on a "trial and error" basis. Nobody is interested in burned bread....

Anybody can do this business; preparation however "is King"

A successful Direct Seller is somebody who has an interesting story to tell and has credibility. Self-discipline and personal work ethics are key strengths you will want to develop.

Make a list of people you know is your one of the basics. It is effective and fast to share your opportunity with your contacts.

The social networks on internet (Facebook, LinkedIn, and Twitter) are another source of contacts.

Fact: The average person connects with 100+ people.

Personal Development

To succeed in Direct Selling, you must develop YOU. To increase your chances of success in anything, you must continually **grow** as a person, and learn the communication skills necessary to achieve **your** goals.

Your business is about you and what you can and will make of your opportunity. People who are attracted to Direct Selling tend to be more open to changes.

Of all the components of your home-based business, the one you must sharpen and develop daily is you, the Entrepreneur and Business Owner. It's fun and rewarding to do so!

Therefore, Top Earners advice you to go to meetings and conventions.

Conventions & Meetings

This business is built on belief in yourself and your ability to do it. **Conventions and meetings are fun and essential to follow as this will allow you to get the big picture!**

Many have turned to direct selling to make their business dreams come true.

You will get energized, focused and will learn tons of strategies to accomplish more and faster on a regional, national or international convention or a local meeting.

Top Earners are attending meetings, so it would be smart to connect with them and learn from experienced leaders. Conventions and meetings are the place to be!

Sponsoring

Sponsoring is taking personal responsibility for the new participants in the business.

Ensuring that they have a good understanding of the responsibilities associated with owning their own business.

Educating them about the product and mentoring them along the way as they make sales and sponsor other participants.

Sponsoring creates a win/win relationship between the sponsor and the enrollee.

Direct Selling Due Diligence

Due Diligence is a term used to look more into depth in an opportunity. Get some specific information about the company you would like to work with. Information to be obtained could be:

Who is the owner / CEO?_____

When did the Company start? _____

Is the company debt free?_____

Is it a member of the Direct Selling Organization? _____

Is it a member of the Better Business Bureau?_____

Who is your up line?_____

Do you get a free (replicated) website?_____

Is customer / distributor support in place?_____

Does the company do the shipping and handling?_____

Does the company have a buy back policy?_____

Who is the Nr.1 earner?_____

What is the minimum investment to start?_____

What is the start up package cost?_____

This questions answered will help make a well informed decision thus better prepared to start fast and be successful!

Top Earner Suggestions

- Connect with Top Earners; they love to share knowledge and to guide you.
- Follow trainings and webinars, Top Earners do. It is the key to success and motivation.

- If you have a bad day, watch a motivational video.

- Be positive, it always benefits your business.
- Build a relationship first, do not jump on people.
- More people will join you if you lead by example.

- Don't try to explain the marketing plan on a street corner.
- Make a friend and meet their friends.
- The majority of the Top Earners are introduced by newbie's, so do not judge people.

- If you have an EGO throw it away, it is an expensive, bad habit and nobody likes it.
- Take a "no "with a smile, you never know if somebody will change his or her mind.

- Dress for success, it gives you more credibility.
- You don't have to understand the compensation plan all the way. The basics will do.

- **Connect with nice people, result will follow.**

Famous One Liners

- You are never too old to get started.
- You get paid to be friendly.

- Action may not always bring happiness, but there is no happiness without action.
- The average Top Earner makes $20,000+ a month.
- Direct Selling is the greatest gift you can give.

- If you want your life to be better, you have to be better.
- Look for positive people, working with negative people is no fun.
- Do you have an open mind?
- KISS, Keep It Simple Stupid.
- Success is a choice.
- Grow fast, earn more.

- Build local, grow global.
- If you start judging people, you will be having no time to love them.
- If you are the biggest fish in the pool, you need to find another pool, you don't grow!

10 Keys to Success

1. Have a positive attitude

2. Set your goal

3. Build a contact list

4. Take action

5. Work with positive people

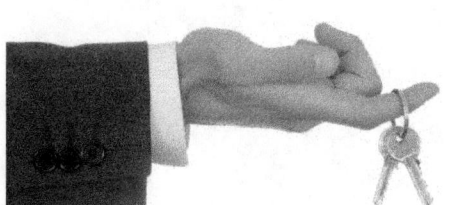

6. Share your product or service

7. Share the opportunity

8. Promote the events

9. Develop your skills

10. Duplicate

Top 300*

Nr.	Name	Company	Country	Est. Month	Est. Year
1	Lita & Brig Hart	Monavie	USA	$950,000	$11,400,000
2	Barry Chi & Holly Chen	Amway	Taiwan	$850,000	$10,200,000
3	Mike Dillard	Magnetic Sp.	USA	$592,000	$7,104,000
4	George Zalucki & Art N.	ACN	USA	$475,000	$5,700,000
5	Howe Kean	Amway	Malaysia	$450,000	$5,400,000
6	Enrique & Gr. Varela	Herbalife	USA	$425,000	$5,100,000
7	Carol & Ken Porter	Monavie	USA	$400,000	$4,800,000
8	Sunny Su	Amway	Taiwan	$400,000	$4,800,000
9	Rolf Kipp	FLP	Germany	$375,000	$4,500,000
10	Bill & Peggy Britt	Amway	USA	$350,000	$4,200,000
11	Dexter Yager	Amway	USA	$350,000	$4,200,000
12	Gina & Steve Merritt	Monavie	USA	$350,000	$4,200,000
13	Jim & Nancy Dornan	Amway	USA	$350,000	$4,200,000
14	Max Schwarz	Amway	Germany	$350,000	$4,200,000
15	Peter & Eva Muller	Amway	Germany	$350,000	$4,200,000
16	Sharon & Steven Sharif	Xango	USA	$350,000	$4,200,000
17	Tsuyoshi Tomioka	Synergy	Japan	$350,000	$4,200,000
18	Charlie & Debbie Kalb	Monavie	USA	$340,000	$4,080,000
19	Debbie & Geoff Davis	ACN	USA	$300,000	$3,600,000
20	Jay Kubassek	CCC	USA	$300,000	$3,600,000
21	John Peterson	Herbalife	USA	$300,000	$3,600,000
22	Kaoru Nakajima	Amway	Japan	$300,000	$3,600,000
23	Marco & Mil. Dubon	FLP	Guatemala	$300,000	$3,600,000
24	Simon Abboud	ACN	USA	$300,000	$3,600,000
25	Susan Peterson	Herbalife	USA	$300,000	$3,600,000
26	Holton Buggs	Organo Gold	USA	$254,000	$3,048,000
27	Brian & Andrea Sax	ACN	USA	$250,000	$3,000,000
28	Dave Johnson	Nikken	USA	$250,000	$3,000,000
29	Jeff Roberti	NSA	USA	$250,000	$3,000,000
30	Kang Hyeon Sook	Amway	Korea	$250,000	$3,000,000

Updated ranks see: www.businessforhome.org

Top 300

Nr.	Name	Company	Country	Est. Month	Est. Year
31	Leonard & Esther Kim	Amway	Korea	$250,000	$3,000,000
32	Mark & Peggy Lei	Amway	Taiwan	$250,000	$3,000,000
33	Onyx Coale	Monavie	USA	$250,000	$3,000,000
34	Patrick Maser	ACN	USA	$250,000	$3,000,000
35	Roberto Ruiz	FLP	Mexico	$250,000	$3,000,000
36	Jennifer & Darin Dowd	ACN	USA	$225,000	$2,700,000
37	Leonard & Esther Kim	Amway	Korea	$225,000	$2,700,000
38	Shane & Dana Douglas	ACN	USA	$225,000	$2,700,000
39	Carol & Alan Lorrenz	Herbalife	USA	$220,000	$2,640,000
40	Corbin & Holly Roush	Monavie	USA	$220,000	$2,640,000
41	Chris Carley	Herbalife	USA	$200,000	$2,400,000
42	Danny Bae	ACN	USA	$200,000	$2,400,000
43	Ed Bestoso	Melaleuca	USA	$200,000	$2,400,000
44	Giselle Sexsmith	Nu Skin	Puerto Rico	$200,000	$2,400,000
45	Markus Lehmann	Herbalife	Germany	$200,000	$2,400,000
46	Natalya Yena	Amway	Russia	$200,000	$2,400,000
47	Rick Jordan	Unicity	USA	$200,000	$2,400,000
48	Sherman Unkefer	Xango	USA	$200,000	$2,400,000
49	Daniel Mueller	Unicity	Germany	$180,000	$2,160,000
50	Jordan Adler	Send Out C.	USA	$176,000	$2,112,000
51	Jeff Weber	ACN	USA	$175,000	$2,100,000
52	Keith McEachern	FreeLife	USA	$175,000	$2,100,000
53	Mitch & Deidre Sala	Amway	USA	$175,000	$2,100,000
54	Sven Goebel	Unicity	Germany	$175,000	$2,100,000
55	Tom & Bet. Alkazin	Vemma	USA	$175,000	$2,100,000
56	Dave Savula	Pre Paid L.	USA	$166,000	$1,992,000
57	Margie Aliprandi	Neways	USA	$165,000	$1,980,000
58	Dominique Cano-Flores	ACN	France	$160,000	$1,920,000
59	Jonathan Budd	MLM S.	USA	$160,000	$1,920,000
60	Rita Hui	USANA	Hong Kong	$160,000	$1,920,000

Updated ranks see: www.businessforhome.org

Top 300

Nr.	Name	Company	Country	Est. Month	Est. Year
61	Ruth & Jeff Elliot	Vemma	USA	$155,000	$1,860,000
62	Steve & Melyn Campbell	Exfuze	USA	$153,000	$1,836,000
63	Carsten Ledule	PM Intern.	Germany	$152,858	$1,834,296
64	Brian McClure	Ambit Energy	USA	$151,000	$1,812,000
65	Art & Terry Manville	Xango	USA	$150,000	$1,800,000
66	Collette Larsen	USANA	USA	$150,000	$1,800,000
67	Craig Bryson	Nu Skin	USA	$150,000	$1,800,000
68	Darrell & Tr. Utterbach	Monavie	USA	$150,000	$1,800,000
69	Eimerl & Herrick & Rose	ACN	USA	$150,000	$1,800,000
70	Geri Cvitanovich	Herbalife	USA	$150,000	$1,800,000
71	Jeremy & Mindy Deeble	ACN	USA	$150,000	$1,800,000
72	Kenny Rossi	Nikken	USA	$150,000	$1,800,000
73	Maria Schleipfer & W.	Amway	Germany	$150,000	$1,800,000
74	Ron & Br. Prudhomme	Monavie	USA	$150,000	$1,800,000
75	Scott & Sue Olsen	Monavie	USA	$150,000	$1,800,000
76	Spencer Hunn	ACN	USA	$150,000	$1,800,000
77	Steve Thompson	Ambit Energy	USA	$150,000	$1,800,000
78	Tim & Kristin Sharif	Xango	USA	$150,000	$1,800,000
79	Tim Foley	Amway	USA	$150,000	$1,800,000
80	Zachary Ross	USANA	USA	$150,000	$1,800,000
81	Ken Dunn	Max Intern.	USA	$148,000	$1,776,000
82	Geoff Libermann	Euphony	UK	$146,000	$1,752,000
83	Ahuva Simone	Nikken	Canada	$140,000	$1,680,000
84	Katrin Bajri	FLP	Germany	$140,000	$1,680,000
85	Orrin Woodward	Monavie	USA	$140,000	$1,680,000
86	Dianne & Lorin Leavitt	Synergy	USA	$130,000	$1,560,000
87	Elizabeth Weber	Market Am.	USA	$130,000	$1,560,000
88	Jimmy Smith	Isagenix	USA	$130,000	$1,560,000
89	Mac McDonald	Nikken	USA	$130,000	$1,560,000
90	Mark Comer	Synergy	USA	$130,000	$1,560,000

Updated ranks see: www.businessforhome.org

Top 300

Rank	Name	Company	Est. Month	Est. Year
91	Michaël P. Hamilton	Herbalife	$130,000	$1,560,000
92	Rafael Rojas	Melaleuca	$130,000	$1,560,000
93	Steve & Leigh Little	WorldVentures	$130,000	$1,560,000
94	Presley & Jeanie Swagerty	Ignite	$127,000	$1,524,000
95	Franco LoFranco	ACN	$125,000	$1,500,000
96	Ronald & Bea Bos	Herbalife	$125,000	$1,500,000
97	Todd & Angelique Hartog	Monavie	$125,000	$1,500,000
98	Eric Worre	Agel	$120,000	$1,440,000
99	Greg Tedrow	Noni	$120,000	$1,440,000
100	Jack Firestone	Liberty League	$120,000	$1,440,000
101	Jeff & Maureen Miller	Melaleuca	$120,000	$1,440,000
102	Jurgen Liebig	LR	$120,000	$1,440,000
103	Mike Bisutti	ACN	$120,000	$1,440,000
104	John & Jana Haremza	Waiora	$118,000	$1,416,000
105	Brian Carruthers	Pre Paid Legal	$116,000	$1,392,000
106	Chanida Puranaputra	Agel	$115,000	$1,380,000
107	Logan & Haley Stout	Ignite	$114,000	$1,368,000
108	Anton Bonde	Nu Skin	$110,000	$1,320,000
109	Brian & Jill Cattano	Monavie	$110,000	$1,320,000
110	Eddy & Grace Chai	FLP	$110,000	$1,320,000
111	Randy Gage	Agel	$110,000	$1,320,000
112	Alan Pariser	Melaleuca	$106,000	$1,272,000
113	Matt Morris	WorldVentures	$106,000	$1,272,000
114	Niti Sawangsap	Agel	$103,000	$1,236,000
115	Jeremy & Karen Reynolds	Xocai	$101,000	$1,212,000
116	Bill & Cindy Anderson	Max International	$100,000	$1,200,000
117	Bo Sundberg	Unicity	$100,000	$1,200,000
118	Chan Koon Tin	Amway	$100,000	$1,200,000
119	Chan Lee Sean	Amway	$100,000	$1,200,000
120	Chen Tsai Lung	Amway	$100,000	$1,200,000

Updated ranks see: www.businessforhome.org

Top 300

Nr.	Name	Company	Est. Month	Est. Year
121	Chin Nai Kang & Wang Shu Chen	Amway	$100,000	$1,200,000
122	Clement & Anita Fu	Amway	$100,000	$1,200,000
123	Craig & Chelsea Kotter	ACN	$100,000	$1,200,000
124	Deng Feng Hua & Hu Tian Peng	Amway	$100,000	$1,200,000
125	Dick & Sandee Marks	Amway	$100,000	$1,200,000
126	Domo Kovacevic	ACN	$100,000	$1,200,000
127	E.H. Erick & Ito Midori	Amway	$100,000	$1,200,000
128	Enrique Javier Varela Mier	Herbalife	$100,000	$1,200,000
129	Gabi Steiner	Lifeplus	$100,000	$1,200,000
130	Han Shi Rong	Amway	$100,000	$1,200,000
131	Hidekazu & Yuki Kajihara	Amway	$100,000	$1,200,000
132	Hyeon Sook & Ryu In Ik Kang	Amway	$100,000	$1,200,000
133	Johnson & Jennifer Tu	Amway	$100,000	$1,200,000
134	Khoo Chong Kok & Chai Choo	Amway	$100,000	$1,200,000
135	Kwon HwaJa & Jo Kyu Seong	Amway	$100,000	$1,200,000
136	Lee Tong Cheol	Amway	$100,000	$1,200,000
137	LK Marketing	Pre Paid L.	$100,000	$1,200,000
138	Lyndon Redman	USANA	$100,000	$1,200,000
139	Mautanov Vira	Amway	$100,000	$1,200,000
140	Maxime Butera	ACN	$100,000	$1,200,000
141	Mikio & Yuka Kaku	Amway	$100,000	$1,200,000
142	Morihiko & Seiko Kitakon	Amway	$100,000	$1,200,000
143	Nanae & Seisuke Arima	Amway	$100,000	$1,200,000
144	Nathan Ricks	Nu Skin	$100,000	$1,200,000
145	Paula Pritchard	Xocai	$100,000	$1,200,000
146	Peter & Choi Kit Lee	Amway	$100,000	$1,200,000
147	Robert & Ranti Angkasa	Amway	$100,000	$1,200,000
148	Ryusuke & Elaine Seto	Amway	$100,000	$1,200,000
149	Shizunori & Mieko Yamamoto	Amway	$100,000	$1,200,000
150	Sonny & Guat Hwa Ho	Amway	$100,000	$1,200,000

Updated ranks see: www.businessforhome.org

Top 300

Nr.	Name	Company	Est. Month	Est. Year
151	Soomboon Khunkhlai	Amway	$100,000	$1,200,000
152	Spencer & Leanna Hunn	ACN	$100,000	$1,200,000
153	Takeshi & Hidemi Azumi	Amway	$100,000	$1,200,000
154	Taras & Irina Demkura	Amway	$100,000	$1,200,000
155	Tetsuya Shibatomi	Neways	$100,000	$1,200,000
156	Tish Rochin	Herbalife	$100,000	$1,200,000
157	Toshiaki & Tomoko Takahashi	Amway	$100,000	$1,200,000
158	Totsuo & Atsuke Hayashi	Amway	$100,000	$1,200,000
159	Viroah & Siriphan Boonariya	Amway	$100,000	$1,200,000
160	William & Roslyn Francis	Synergy	$100,000	$1,200,000
161	Xian Xing Lu	Amway	$100,000	$1,200,000
162	Yoshiko Hatayama Kenichiro	Amway	$100,000	$1,200,000
163	Yoshiyuki & Mineko Yamazaki	Amway	$100,000	$1,200,000
164	Zheng Wei Liang & Luo Bin	Amway	$100,000	$1,200,000
165	Joe & Patrice Licciardi	Monavie	$95,000	$1,140,000
166	Dean & Angie Mannheimer	DUBLI	$90,000	$1,080,000
167	Dennis Estes	Nikken	$90,000	$1,080,000
168	Hak-Soo Jeong	Amway	$90,000	$1,080,000
169	In-Geon Kwon	Amway	$90,000	$1,080,000
170	In-Soo Jang & Hyo-Ji Kim	Amway	$90,000	$1,080,000
171	Jack & Ying Zhou	Amway	$90,000	$1,080,000
172	Jae-Oh Joo & Kyung-Ja Park	Amway	$90,000	$1,080,000
173	Jeff Hooks	Vemma	$90,000	$1,080,000
174	Jintana & Witat Pornjaded	Amway	$90,000	$1,080,000
175	Ken Roland	Noni	$90,000	$1,080,000
176	Lee Kim Soon & Kwee Choo	Amway	$90,000	$1,080,000
177	Michael Force	CCP	$90,000	$1,080,000
178	Pete Pena	Liberty L.	$90,000	$1,080,000
179	Peter & Debbie Cox	Amway	$90,000	$1,080,000
180	Renata Lee	Isagenix	$90,000	$1,080,000

Updated ranks see: www.businessforhome.org

Top 300

Nr.	Name	Company	Est. Month	Est. Year
181	Steven Thompson	Zrii	$90,000	$1,080,000
182	Sun Dong & Liang Ding Su	Amway	$90,000	$1,080,000
183	Takumi & Rieko Yamazaki	Amway	$90,000	$1,080,000
184	Tomoko & Shuji Hamamoto	Amway	$90,000	$1,080,000
185	Vira Arkhipova	Amway	$90,000	$1,080,000
186	Zhou Wan Ming	Amway	$90,000	$1,080,000
187	Benjamin Ginder	Market Am.	$89,000	$1,068,000
188	Joanne Hsi	Market Am.	$89,000	$1,068,000
189	Ming Chukuo	Market Am.	$89,000	$1,068,000
190	Amy & Tim Marks	Monavie	$85,000	$1,020,000
191	Andre & Penny Walton	Monavie	$85,000	$1,020,000
192	Anthony & Megan Wolf.	Monavie	$85,000	$1,020,000
193	Bob & Linda Robinson	Monavie	$85,000	$1,020,000
194	Brian & Jacqueline Thayer	Monavie	$85,000	$1,020,000
195	Calvin Becerra	Monavie	$85,000	$1,020,000
196	Carrie & Bo van Pelt	Monavie	$85,000	$1,020,000
197	Carrie & Godon Dickie	Monavie	$85,000	$1,020,000
198	Carrie & Jason Lyons	Monavie	$85,000	$1,020,000
199	Chris & Terri Brady	Monavie	$85,000	$1,020,000
200	Devon Robinson	Monavie	$85,000	$1,020,000
201	Dickie Clan	Monavie	$85,000	$1,020,000
202	Ed & Shelly Aristizábal	Monavie	$85,000	$1,020,000
203	Eric & Rebekah Gutman	Monavie	$85,000	$1,020,000
204	Franck & Tina Dupart	Monavie	$85,000	$1,020,000
205	Frank & Cindy Sounicek	Monavie	$85,000	$1,020,000
206	Grayson Maule	Monavie	$85,000	$1,020,000
207	Jill & Mark Ewell	Monavie	$85,000	$1,020,000
208	John & Barbara Sims	Monavie	$85,000	$1,020,000
209	Kathleen Deggelman	Monavie	$85,000	$1,020,000
210	Linda & Bob Robinson	Monavie	$85,000	$1,020,000

Updated ranks see: www.businessforhome.org

Top 300

Nr.	Name	Company	Est. Month	Est. Year
211	Mark & Tami Crawford	Monavie	$85,000	$1,020,000
212	Matthew & Kimberly Curtis	Monavie	$85,000	$1,020,000
213	Penny & Andre Walton	Monavie	$85,000	$1,020,000
214	Phil & Jennifer Sack	Monavie	$85,000	$1,020,000
215	Rob & Lisa Alwin	Monavie	$85,000	$1,020,000
216	Rodney & Adonica Howard-Br.	Monavie	$85,000	$1,020,000
217	Rodney Howard	Monavie	$85,000	$1,020,000
218	Ronn & Janich Prpich	Monavie	$85,000	$1,020,000
219	Sandra & Angel Matos	Monavie	$85,000	$1,020,000
220	Sheree & Steven Burton	Monavie	$85,000	$1,020,000
221	Stephanie & Todd Smith	Monavie	$85,000	$1,020,000
222	Teresa & Scott Henry	Monavie	$85,000	$1,020,000
223	Tim Wilson	Monavie	$85,000	$1,020,000
224	Vick & Mick Karshner	Monavie	$85,000	$1,020,000
225	Mark Brown	Pre Paid Legal	$83,000	$996,000
226	Nick & Gayle Serba	Pre Paid Legal	$83,000	$996,000
227	Carole Taylor	Isagenix	$80,000	$960,000
228	Clay Jackson	Vemma	$80,000	$960,000
229	Dave & Joyce Jordan	Waiora	$80,000	$960,000
230	David & Colli Butler	Xango	$80,000	$960,000
231	Leon & Irana Waisbein	Herbalife	$80,000	$960,000
232	Stephan & Gaura Gratziani	Herbalife	$80,000	$960,000
233	Tom Wood	Genewize	$80,000	$960,000
234	Raven K Starre	Monavie	$75,200	$902,400
235	Alexander Krause	Unicity	$75,000	$900,000
236	Andrew Cass	CarbonCopyPro	$75,000	$900,000
237	Anna Kagan	Nikken	$75,000	$900,000
238	Arie & Ilana Baratz	Herbalife	$75,000	$900,000
239	Blake Morgan	Herbalife	$75,000	$900,000
240	Bryan & Monica Penrod	USANA	$75,000	$900,000

Updated ranks see: www.businessforhome.org

Top 300

Nr.	Name	Company	Est. Month	Est. Year
241	Chang Mo & Ok Kyung Park	Herbalife	$75,000	$900,000
242	Darnell & Traci Self	Pre Paid L.	$75,000	$900,000
243	Don Wilson	Amway	$75,000	$900,000
244	Eduardo Salazar	Herbalife	$75,000	$900,000
245	Henria & Stania Smek	Herbalife	$75,000	$900,000
246	Hubert Krause & Seta Der Ar.	USANA	$75,000	$900,000
247	Janifer Cohn	Herbalife	$75,000	$900,000
248	Jennifer Bates & Garry Deb.	Herbalife	$75,000	$900,000
249	John & Lori Tartol	Herbalife	$75,000	$900,000
250	Jose Paulo Dinis & Natalia Fer.	Herbalife	$75,000	$900,000
251	Juan & Hilda Najera	Herbalife	$75,000	$900,000
252	Kuniko Hida	Herbalife	$75,000	$900,000
253	Kurt & Cindy O'Connell	Herbalife	$75,000	$900,000
254	Lee & Lisa Sharif	Xango	$75,000	$900,000
255	Leslie Stanford	Herbalife	$75,000	$900,000
256	Ma Luisa Mier	Herbalife	$75,000	$900,000
257	Martin & Yvonne Ernst	Herbalife	$75,000	$900,000
258	Mathieu Lamontagne	ACN	$75,000	$900,000
259	Micheko DeJaeghere	Herbalife	$75,000	$900,000
260	Molly Yang & Ming-Jei Chen	Herbalife	$75,000	$900,000
261	Natalia Ferreira	Herbalife	$75,000	$900,000
262	Nathan Goldberg	ACN	$75,000	$900,000
263	Pedro & Juliane Cardoso	Herbalife	$75,000	$900,000
264	Queenie Leung	Herbalife	$75,000	$900,000
265	Rick Setzer	Amway	$75,000	$900,000
266	Susanne & John Cunningham	USANA	$75,000	$900,000
267	Trina & Donte Andry	Herbalife	$75,000	$900,000
268	Jeff Bracken	Exfuze	$72,000	$864,000
269	Ben Sturtevant	Lightyear Wire.	$71,000	$852,000
270	Adam & Melannie Green	Xocai	$70,000	$840,000

Updated ranks see: www.businessforhome.org

Top 300

Nr.	Name	Company	Est. Month	Est. Year
271	Al Gardiner	Euphony	$70,000	$840,000
272	Connie Yao & Jim Barabe	USANA	$70,000	$840,000
273	Craig Bailey & Dixie Sounness	Nu Skin	$70,000	$840,000
274	Graham & Frances Park	Nu Skin	$70,000	$840,000
275	Harald Maier	Vemma	$70,000	$840,000
276	Jack Zufelt	Dna of Succes	$70,000	$840,000
277	Kari & Lisha Schneider	WorldVentures	$70,000	$840,000
278	Marcy Littlejohn	Waiora	$70,000	$840,000
279	Matt Morrow	Vemma	$70,000	$840,000
280	Richard Vincenti	Traverus	$70,000	$840,000
281	Sharon Peterman	Herbalife	$70,000	$840,000
282	Dolly Kuo	Market America	$68,000	$816,000
283	Frank Keefer	Market America	$68,000	$816,000
284	Patrick & Alice Hsieh & Chen	Market America	$68,000	$816,000
285	Victor & Alice Chiou	Market America	$68,000	$816,000
286	Jeff Street & Janet Thacker	ACN	$67,000	$804,000
287	Amertat Cohn	Herbalife	$65,000	$780,000
288	Bin Yang	USANA	$65,000	$780,000
289	Dan & Rebecca Brink	USANA	$65,000	$780,000
290	Daniel & Paige Hunter	USANA	$65,000	$780,000
291	Edgardo Valdivieso	Xango	$65,000	$780,000
292	Ejder & Goknur Inam	Herbalife	$65,000	$780,000
293	Gregg Davidson	CarbonCopyPro	$65,000	$780,000
294	Martyn & Karen Farmer	Herbalife	$65,000	$780,000
295	Wen Chi Wu	USANA	$65,000	$780,000
296	Ata Mamedov	Agel	$62,300	$747,600
297	Matt Rasmussen	ACN	$62,000	$744,000
298	Aaron Rashkin	CarbonCopyPro	$60,000	$720,000
299	Alberto Zirlinger	Agel	$60,000	$720,000
300	Barry Donalson	5Linx	$60,000	$720,000

Updated ranks see: www.businessforhome.org

Recommendations

Paula Pritcha, Xocai

"Direct Selling made simple that is what it is all about"

Steve & Melyn Campbell, Exfuze

" We love this book and what Ted Nuyten is trying to do for our direct sales and network marketing industry. We need more documentation like this, as it lends so much credibility to what we are trying to accomplish. We always like to say that documentation ends conversation and a tool like this book always helps!"

Mike Dillard, Magnetic Sponsoring

"I really love the work Ted Nuyten and his team is putting into this book. It's something everyone wonders about, but few really know. It's a great way to demonstrate what's possible in our industry...."

Matt Morris, World Ventures

"Great book! Very useful information, credible facts & figures"

Jonathan Budd, online mlm secrets

"Awesome book. Facts speak louder then opinions! And clearly this industry is a beacon of hope and light for individuals looking to create an amazing lifestyle, income, and freedom through hard work. Many others are doing it, you can too!".

Tom Alkazin, Vemma

"This book is a great introduction into Direct Selling!"

James Christiansen, Xowii

"Finally an amazing UNBIAS book that is truly a great tool for the industry,with accurate information

Tom Chenault, Home Based Business Radio Show

Great book, I recommend to use it"!

Tom Wood, Genewize

" Ted Nuyten has by far the most extensively researched leader database on Network Marketing companies and leaders I've ever seen.

Rod Cook, Global MLM Watchdog & Founder Distributor Rights Association

"Ted has written a great Direct Selling book that covers all areas of Direct Selling recruitment"

I just love Ted's style in running probably the best MLM Website on the Internet. It looks 100 x better than my MLMWatchdog.com! Ted is always on a hunt to find new positive things to publish about how good MLM is. The MLM industry needs that "Good News" spread around (LIKE TED DOES)

Oh top of that, Ted is not afraid to attack scam artists and crooks that prey on innocent Networkers.

Ted has endured vicious Internet attacks on his website (Dos attacks) and still came back fighting. In the realm of Global Network Marketers Ted should get a big 3 foot high GOLD award for "Top Gun" for protecting and loving the Network Market industry!

Disclaimer

*The estimated earnings are based on Internet research, earnings claims from conventions, down line, up line, cross line information, direct selling magazines and through our reporters. These leaders had an incredible vision, empower people, and change their life through this business.

They build Million-Dollar Distributorships through Million Dollar Relationships. The estimated (gross) earnings are per month and per year. The information contained in this book is for general information purposes only.

While we endeavor to keep the information up to date and correct, we make no representations or warranties of any kind, express or implied, about the completeness, accuracy, reliability, suitability or availability with respect to the content or the information, products, services, or related graphics contained on the book for any purpose.

In no event will we be liable for any loss or damage including without limitation, indirect or consequential loss or damage, or any loss or damage whatsoever arising from loss of data or profits arising out of, or in connection with, the use of this book.

www.ingramcontent.com/pod-product-compliance
Lightning Source LLC
Chambersburg PA
CBHW051258170526
45165CB00004B/1759